Thank you to our readers: you are supporting a wonderful cause

TABLE OF CONTENTS

* all recipes in this cookbook serve 6

Our Story

Mouna: I started cooking when I was 12 years old. My mother taught me everything. We had a big family and lunches were shared with everyone, so it was important for me to learn to cook in order to help my mother. After spending one month in the kitchen with my mother, I had all of her recipes in my head and I was cooking meals from my memory which is the way I still cook today. At lunch, I was cooking for my brothers and their wives and children, my parents, my aunts, and uncles, and I loved it. I loved that my cooking made people happy, I loved that I could do something so special for my family. My special dish was a sweet semolina pudding, I would prepare it and then chill it in the fridge. After cooking in a hot kitchen, it was so nice to have something sweet and cool.

In my village in Syria, my entire family lived nearby. We had very large gardens attached to our homes and all our houses were connected by our gardens. We went to small supermarkets for meat and some other essentials but all the vegetables we needed we grew at home. This is one of the reasons I love vegetables and vegetarian cooking so much! A typical day is a light breakfast and light dinner, but lunch is a huge affair with 30 or 40 family members. My mother and I would cook for everyone and then we all enjoyed our lunch together.

Khaled's story is very different. He learned to cook in a café in Lebanon, simple and quick food. He needed the work but once he started learning to cook, he realised he enjoyed it and was very good at it and he quickly found a better job in a restaurant. Khaled's boss in the restaurant was so pleased to have him but Khaled made such a name for himself that he was offered a visa to go and cook at an upmarket restaurant in Dubai. He loved his experience in Dubai and the restaurant there wanted him to stay but after such a long time, he returned to Syria to be with us. Now he's in Sevenoaks, making people happy with his food. He's been around the world cooking and learning and nourishing his communities. Khaled loves to make hummus and falafel. He makes a large portion of hummus to keep in the fridge and eat whenever we need a snack. We have a tradition, on Fridays, where we have a special big Syrian breakfast with the hummus and his falafel. It is so very delicious!

We hope you enjoy these flavours from our homeland, find your passion for cooking this delicious and healthy food, and share it with your family and friends, just as we enjoy sharing it with ours!

Mouna and Khaled

salads

Syrian Chef Salad

INGREDIENTS:

3 medium tomatoes

1 head of Romaine lettuce

3 stalks of mint

10 black olives

100g feta cheese

3 tbsp olive oil

2 tbsp lemon juice

salt and oregano to taste

WHAT TO DO:

1. Cut the tomatoes, lettuce, mint, olives and feta cheese into small pieces and mix well.

2. Season with olive oil, lemon, salt and oregano.

Aubergine Pickles

INGREDIENTS:

6 long, white aubergines

2 large garlic cloves, crushed

1 red chilli, hot or medium heat

1/2 tsp dry coriander

3 tsp paprika

salt as desired

To cover the aubergine: 1L cold water, 3 tsp salt and 1/2 tsp sugar

WHAT TO DO:

1. Wash the aubergines with cold water, leaving the stalk.

2. Mix all the spices well.

3. Using a sharp knife, make a cut lengthways in the aubergines and boil in hot water for 10 minutes.

4. Drain the water, divide the spices evenly between the 6 aubergines and then rub the inside of the aubergines well with the spices.

5. Arrange the stuffed aubergines in a large jar.

6. Dissolve salt and sugar in a litre of cold water.

7. Cover the stuffed aubergines with the water mix. Place it in the fridge for 7 days before consuming.

Cucumber and Yoghurt Salad

INGREDIENTS:

1kg plain yoghurt

1 whole cucumber

1 clove garlic, crushed

1 tsp dried mint

1 tsp salt

WHAT TO DO:

1. Cut the cucumber into small pieces and put in a serving bowl.

2. Sprinkle with salt and leave for 1 hour.

3. Add yoghurt and garlic to the cucumber and mix well.

4. Sprinkle with dried mint to finish.

"We love to eat this salad in the hot summer months. If you feel too hot to eat, you can have just a little bit of this. It's very refreshing and it tastes wonderful with rice and bulgur dishes and grilled vegetables."

Hummus Dip

INGREDIENTS:

500g dried or tinned large chickpeas

250ml tahini

1 tsp bicarbonate soda

1 tsp salt

1 tbsp lemon juice

3 cloves garlic, crushed

"Hummus goes with everything. It's good in hot weather and it's hearty enough for a cold winters day. It's easy to make and you can make large portions and store in the fridge to eat over several days. It's a very healthy snack to have in your fridge."

WHAT TO DO:

1. If using dried chickpeas, cover with water and leave to soak overnight. However, if using tinned chickpeas, skip to step 2.

2. Drain the water, put the chickpeas in a pan and add water and bicarbonate soda.

3. Cover with lid and leave to cook on a medium heat for 30 minutes or until softened.

4. Drain the water and put the chickpeas in a food processor. Add the rest of the ingredients, blend until smooth.

5. Transfer to a flat dish and drizzle with olive oil.

Maqdous

INGREDIENTS:

1kg small aubergines

1L olive oil

a pinch of salt

For filling:

2 tbsp paprika

½ tsp coriander powder

100g walnut or cashews or mixture of both, chopped into small pieces

WHAT TO DO:

1. Place the aubergines, including the stalks, in a deep pan.

2. Cover with water and place a heatproof plate on top of the aubergines to prevent them from floating.

3. Boil for 20 minutes until the aubergines are soft.

4. Drain the hot water and add cold water to reduce the heat of the aubergines. Leave until they are cool enough to handle.

5. When you can handle the aubergines, make a slit down the centre of each one.

6. Sprinkle salt on the flesh of the aubergines, then place them in a colander and cover with a plate to press them down. Leave for 6 hours until all the juices have run out.

7. Mix the paprika, coriander and nuts, and then stuff the aubergines with the mixture.

8. Arrange the stuffed aubergines in a jar and cover with olive oil.

9. Close the jar tightly and leave in fridge for 7 days before eating.

Note: Maqdous can be kept for about 6 months.

Syrian Veggie Soup

INGREDIENTS:

100g garden peas

100g carrots

2 celery sticks

1 large potato

2 medium courgettes

1 tsp salt

1 tbsp butter

2 cubes vegetable stock

juice of 1 lemon

2 cups water

WHAT TO DO:

1. Prepare the vegetables by cutting into medium-size squares.

2. Melt the butter on low heat and add the prepared vegetables.

3. Add the water, stock and salt and increase the heat to high. Leave to boil.

4. Reduce the heat to medium and leave for 20 minutes or until cooked.

5. Add the lemon juice and turn the heat off.

Vermicelli Soup

INGREDIENTS:

1 cup crushed vermicelli

700ml water

2 cubes vegetable stock

2 tbsp butter

juice of 1 lemon

salt to taste

WHAT TO DO:

1. Melt the butter on low heat and fry the vermicelli until browned.

2. Add water, stock cubes and salt, and increase the heat.

3. Cover and leave to boil for 10 minutes, then add lemon juice.

4. Reduce the heat and cook for another 15 minutes.

sides

Syrian Omelette

INGREDIENTS:

2 bunches flat parsley

6 large eggs

1 medium brown onion, grated or finely diced

250ml vegetable oil

1 tsp each of salt, pepper, paprika and white plain flour

WHAT TO DO:

1. Finely chop the parsley.

2. Whisk the eggs with the salt, pepper and paprika.

3. Add the onion, parsley and flour to the egg mixture and mix well.

4. Heat the oil in a frying pan until sizzling. Scoop a ladle of egg mixture to the middle of the pan.

5. Smooth out in the pan and cook for 3 minutes before flipping. Each side should be golden brown.

Most Delicious Syrian Falafel

INGREDIENTS:

500g dried chickpeas or
400g tin of chickpeas

6 cloves garlic

1 large brown onion

1L vegetable oil

1 tsp mixed spices; dried
coriander, cumin, paprika,
salt and bicarbonate of soda

WHAT TO DO:

1. Soak the chickpeas in a bowl of cold water overnight. If possible, drain and refresh the water a few times.

2. In a food processor, blitz the garlic and onion, then mix in the drained chickpeas and mix until you have a smooth paste. If the mixture is too dry, add some cold water.

3. Leave the mixture to rest for 20 minutes.

4. In a deep frying pan add the vegetable oil and leave on medium heat until bubbling.

5. Roll the paste into small balls and fry in the oil until golden brown.

6. Remove from the oil using a slotted spoon and place on kitchen paper to remove the excess oil.

"Falafel is naturally vegetarian and vegan, and they are so wonderful on their own or in a wrap with yoghurt salad, with cucumber and onions or as part of a salad topping. They are also very filling; a few falafels and you are full of energy for many hours."

Moutabal Aubergine

INGREDIENTS:

2 medium aubergines

1 large brown onion, finely chopped

1/2 green pepper, finely chopped

1 tbsp lemon juice

1 tbsp olive oil, salt as desired

pieces of cucumber, tomatoes, and handful of pomegranate seeds for decoration

WHAT TO DO:

1. Prick the aubergines all over with a fork or knife to keep them from exploding in the oven. Roast the aubergine in the oven at 200C until soft.

2. When the aubergines are cool enough to handle, peel the skin and place the flesh in a medium bowl. Mash the flesh until it is a pulp.

3. On the hob, heat oil at a medium heat and fry the onion and pepper until softened, about 5 minutes.

4. Add the mashed aubergines and reduce heat to low. Add lemon juice and salt, and stir together for another 5 minutes.

5. Decorate with slices of cucumber and tomatoes. Scatter pomegranate seeds on top.

Moutabal Shawander

INGREDIENTS:

350g fresh beetroot

100ml plain yoghurt

1 tsp pomegranate molasses

2 tbsp lemon juice

salt as desired and finely chopped parsley to decorate

WHAT TO DO:

1. Boil the beetroot until tender.

2. Peel the beetroot skin, roughly chop the flesh or use a food processor to create a coarse mash.

3. Add yoghurt, lemon juice, salt and pomegranate molasses to the beetroot, and mix all ingredients well.

4. Place on a serving plate and garnish with chopped parsley.

Fava Beans with Vegetables

INGREDIENTS:

2 400g tins fava beans

2 tbsp tinned chickpeas

1 medium tomato, finely chopped

15 parsley stalks, finely chopped

1/2 cucumber, finely chopped

1 medium red onion, finely chopped

2 stalks of fresh mint leaves

2 tbsp olive oil

1 tbsp fresh lemon juice

salt and pepper as desired

WHAT TO DO:

1. Place fava beans and chickpeas in a saucepan and cover with water. Cook on medium for 10 minutes, stirring continuously.

2. Drain the beans and discard water.

3. Put the beans in a large bowl.

4. Mix into the beans the tomato, cucumber, onion, parsley and mint.

4. Season with olive oil and lemon juice, salt and pepper.

main dishes

Syrian Vegetable Rice

INGREDIENTS:

250g basmati rice

2 cups water

50g each of peas, carrots, and mushroom

1 large red onion, finely chopped

1 medium tomato, finely chopped

2 cubes vegetable stock

1/2 tsp ground turmeric

1/2 tsp baharat, salt and white pepper to taste

2 tbsp vegetable oil

WHAT TO DO:

1. Heat the oil in a pan and add the onion and tomatoes. Cook for 3 minutes, stirring continuously.

2. Add the vegetables, stock, and spices. Stir on low heat for another 5 minutes.

3. Add the water and leave to boil. Add the rice to the mixture and continue to boil for 2 minutes.

4. Reduce the heat and simmer for 30 minutes until cooked.

Serving Suggestion: Serve with Yoghurt Salad (page 8) and Fried Potatoes (page 52).

Courgette and Tomato Stew

INGREDIENTS:

1 large courgette or medium marrow, cut into cubes

750g tomatoes, finely chopped

1 large brown onion, diced

1 tsp salt to taste

1 tsp black pepper

1 tsp paprika

4 tbsp olive oil

WHAT TO DO:

1. Heat the oil in a pan on medium heat and add the onion. Cook for 4 minutes, stirring continuously.

2. Add the courgette and stir together for another 4 minutes.

3. Add tomatoes and the rest of the ingredients. Stir well, cover and cook on medium heat for about 30 minutes.

Serving Suggestion: Serve with rice and Yoghurt Salad (page 8).

Tip: You can use green beans or peas instead of courgette.

Sautéed Green Beans

INGREDIENTS:

1kg green beans, cut diagonally

1 large brown onion, sliced

3 cloves garlic, crushed

2 tbsp lemon juice

1/2 tsp paprika

salt and pepper to taste

4 tbsp vegetable oil

WHAT TO DO:

1. Heat the oil in a pan and add the onion. Cook for 4 minutes, stirring continuously.

2. Add the green beans and stir for another 3 minutes.

3. Add the rest of the ingredients, mix well, reduce the heat, cover and leave for ½ an hour or until cooked.

Serving Suggestion: Serve with Fried Potatoes (page 52) and Syrian Chef Salad (page 4).

Sautéed Spinach with Garlic

INGREDIENTS:

1 kg spinach

1 large brown onion, finely chopped

5 cloves garlic, crushed

3 tbsp lemon juice

1 tsp ground coriander and 1 tsp salt

2 tbsp vegetable oil

WHAT TO DO:

1. Heat the oil in a pan and add the onion. Cook for 5 minutes on low heat, stirring continuously.

2. Add garlic and coriander and mix well with the onion. Cook for 2 minutes.

3. Add spinach, salt and lemon juice, mix well, cover and cook for 20 minutes.

Serving Suggestion: Serve with rice, Moutabal Aubergine (page 20) and Aubergine Pickles (page 5).

Sautéed Chard

INGREDIENTS:

1 kg chard, finely chopped

1 large brown onion, finely chopped

5 cloves garlic, crushed

3 tbsp lemon juice

1 tsp paprika

1 tsp salt and 1/2 tsp pepper

3 tbsp vegetable oil

WHAT TO DO:

1. In a saucepan, cover the chard with hot water and simmer for 10 minutes or until wilted.

2. Drain the chard and set aside.

3. Heat the oil in the pan. Add onions and stir for 5 minutes, or until the onions soften.

4. Add the rest of the ingredients including the chard. Mix well, cover and cook for another 10 minutes or until cooked.

Serving Suggestion: Serve with Bulgur (page 48) and Yoghurt Salad (page 8).

Seasoned Cauliflower Bites

INGREDIENTS:

1 large cauliflower, cut into medium-size florets

1L vegetable oil

2 medium eggs

3 tsp plain white flour

1 tsp ground cumin

1 tsp ground coriander

1 tsp paprika

1 tsp salt and pepper, or to taste

3 tbsp lemon juice

WHAT TO DO:

1. In a medium bowl, whisk the eggs with the spices and salt. Ensure these are mixed well together.

2. Add the water to the flour and lemon juice. Mix well, ensuring the mixture is thick enough to coat the cauliflower.

3. Heat the oil in a frying pan.

4. Coat the florets with the egg mixture and then fry in hot oil until browned.

5. Remove from the oil using slotted spoon. Place on kitchen roll to remove the excess oil.

Serving Suggestion: Serve with Hummus Dip (page 9) and Syrian Chef Salad (page 4).

Raw Kibbeh

INGREDIENTS:

500g medium bulgur wheat

1 tsp dried mint

1 tsp ground cumin

1 tsp ground coriander

1 tsp paprika

1 bundle parsley, finely chopped

salt to taste

WHAT TO DO:

1. Boil the water and season it with all the spices, ensuring there is enough to cover the bulgur.

2. Rub the bulgur with your hands until it sticks together.

3. Add the parsley to the bulgur and rub together until it sticks.

4. Divide the bulgur mixture into equal parts and shape into small egg shapes.

5. On a serving plate, place the kibbeh sauce and arrange the kibbeh on top of the sauce.

TO MAKE THE KIBBEH SAUCE:

1. Finely chop 2 onions and 2 red peppers.

2. In a frying pan add 4 tbsp vegetable oil and heat.

3. Add the onions and peppers and stir. Season with salt and black pepper.

4. Leave to cook on low heat for 15 minutes.

Serving Suggestion: Serve with Syrian Veggie Soup (page 13) and Moutabal Shawander (page 21).

Potatoes with Onion and Tomatoes

INGREDIENTS:

500g peeled potatoes, cut into cubes

500g tomatoes, finely chopped

1 large brown onion, diced

1 tsp salt and black pepper

1 tsp paprika

4 tbsp olive oil

WHAT TO DO:

1. Heat the oil in a pan and add the onion. Cook for 4 minutes, stirring continuously.

2. Add the potatoes and stir together for another 4 minutes.

3. Add tomatoes and the seasonings. Stir, cover and reduce to medium heat and cook for about 30 minutes.

Serving Suggestion: Serve with Falafel (page 17) and Yoghurt Salad (page 8).

Caramelised Mushrooms

INGREDIENTS:

1 kg mushrooms, cut into quarters

2 large brown onions, sliced

2 tsp lemon juice

salt and pepper to taste

3 tbsp vegetable oil

WHAT TO DO:

1. Heat the oil in a frying pan until sizzling.

2. Add onions and stir for 5 minutes until golden brown.

3. Add mushrooms and cook for another 5 minutes. Season with salt, pepper and the lemon juice.

Serving Suggestion: Serve with Egg Omelette (page 16) and Fava Beans with Vegetables (page 24).

Stuffed Peppers

INGREDIENTS:

4 green or yellow peppers

1 medium brown onion, diced

1 medium carrot, finely chopped

1 small tomato, finely chopped

1 tsp chopped parsley and 1 tsp chopped mint

200g long grain rice

2tbsp vegetable oil

salt, pepper and paprika to taste

WHAT TO DO:

1. Soak the rice in boiled water for 30 minutes.

2. Wash and cut the peppers lengthwise. Remove stems, seeds and piths.

3. Mix all the chopped ingredients together in a large bowl.

4. Drain the rice and add to the chopped ingredients.

5. Season with salt, pepper and paprika as desired.

6. Fill each half pepper with the rice mixture and place on an oven tray. Bake for 25 minutes at 160C.

Serving Suggestion: Serve with Fried Potatoes (page 52) and Syrian Chef Salad (page 4).

Stuffed Cabbage Rolls

INGREDIENTS:

1 large white cabbage

250g long grain rice

5 cloves of garlic, crushed

1 large brown onion, finely chopped

1 medium tomato, finely chopped

1 green pepper, finely chopped

a handful each of parsley and mint, finely chopped

1 tsp salt, 1 tsp pepper and 1 tsp paprika

2 tbsp vegetable oil

WHAT TO DO:

1. Soak the cabbage leaves in boiled water until soft, then drain and set aside.

2. Soak rice for 30 minutes, rinse and place in a large bowl. Mix the rest of the ingredients with the rice.

3. Put 1 tbsp of the rice mixture in the centre of each cabbage leaf. Then, fold the sides of the leaf over the mixture and wrap tightly.

4. Arrange all the cabbage rolls in a large, deep-sided pan and cover with hot water, season generously with salt. Cover the cabbage with a plate so that the rolls are completely submerged in the salty water.

5. Cook on low heat for 45 minutes, then remove the plate and add 250ml of pomegranate molasses to the mixture and let rest for 5 minutes.

6. To serve, put a large serving platter over the top of the pan. Quickly and carefully (over a sink is advisable), flip the pan upside down and transfer the cabbage rolls onto the serving platter.

Potatoes with Lemon and Coriander

INGREDIENTS:

500g potatoes

1 large brown onion, chopped

3 cloves garlic, chopped

1 tbsp chopped coriander

2 tbsp lemon juice

2 tbsp vegetable oil

salt and pepper to taste

WHAT TO DO:

1. Peel the potatoes and cut into medium size cubes.

2. Heat the oil in a frying pan and add the chopped onions. Stir for 2 minutes.

3. Add garlic and coriander and stir for another 2 minutes.

4. Add potato cubes, salt and pepper. Stir well and cover the pan.

5. Leave on a medium heat for 25 minutes then add the lemon juice and stir for 3 minutes.

Serving Suggestion: Serve with Moutabal Aubergine (page 20) and Syrian Chef Salad (page 4).

Green Beans

INGREDIENTS:

500g fresh green beans

1 large brown onion, chopped

3 cloves garlic, chopped

salt, pepper and paprika to taste

2 tbsp vegetable oil

WHAT TO DO:

1. Finely chop the green beans.

2. Heat the oil in a pan, add onions and stir for 3 minutes.

3. Add beans and seasoning, stir well and cover. Leave on medium heat and stir every 2 minutes.

4. After 10 minutes add garlic and leave for another 20 minutes or until cooked.

Serving Suggestion: Serve with Fried Potatoes (page 52) and Yoghurt Salad (page 8).

Kawag

INGREDIENTS:

1 large potato

1 large brown onion

1 large carrot

1/2 butternut squash

1 medium aubergine

1 medium courgette

3 tbsp vegetable oil

1 tbsp chili sauce

1 tsp turmeric

1/2 tsp ginger powder

salt and pepper to taste

WHAT TO DO:

1. Chop all the vegetables into large cubes.

2. Mix all the spices together.

3. Place the vegetables in an oven tray and season generously with the mixed spices.

4. Drizzle with oil and bake for 40 minutes at 180C.

Serving Suggestion: Serve with rice and Yoghurt Salad (page 8).

Stuffed Dried Aubergines

INGREDIENTS:

1/2 packet dried aubergine (about 12 pieces), available from Middle Eastern shops

100g long grain rice

1 large brown onion, finely chopped

15 stalks parsley, finely chopped

1 large tomato, finely chopped

5 stalks mint, finely chopped

1/2 green pepper, finely chopped

1 tbsp pomegranate molasses

2 tbsp olive oil

1/2 tsp paprika

salt and pepper as desired

WHAT TO DO:

1. Soak the dried aubergine pieces in boiled water for 5 minutes.

2. Drain the water and prepare the stuffing mixture.

3. Soak rice in warm water to rinse the starch.

4. Add all other ingredients to the rice, and mix well.

5. Fill each aubergine halfway with the rice mixture.

6. Arrange the stuffed aubergines in a medium-size pan.

7. Cover with 1 litre of hot water and the pomegranate molasses, 1 tbsp lemon juice and salt.

8. Cover the aubergines with a flat plate so that they remian submerged. Cover the pan and place on high heat for 20 minutes, then reduce the heat and cook for another 40 minutes.

Serving Suggestion: Serve with Vermicelli Soup (page 14) and Moutabal Shawander (page 21).

Tahini Courgette

INGREDIENTS:

4 large courgettes

2 tbsp tahini

250g plain yoghurt

2 large cloves garlic, crushed

1 tbsp lemon juice

1/2 tsp paprika

salt to taste

WHAT TO DO:

1. Wash the courgettes and cut into thin lengthways pieces.

2. Heat the oil in a frying pan until sizzling.

3. Fry the courgette in the oil until browned.

4. Lift from the oil and place the courgettes on kitchen paper to drain the excess oil.

5. Add tahini, yoghurt, crushed garlic, lemon juice, salt and paprika, and mix well with an electric mixer.

6. Coat the courgettes with the tahini mixture and then arrange on a serving platter.

Serving Suggesion: Serve with Falafel (page 17) and Syrian Chef Salad (page 4).

Manakish

INGREDIENTS:

500g plain flour

1/2 tsp salt

1/2 tsp dry yeast

1 tbsp olive oil

2 tbsp plain yoghurt

100ml warm water

250g mozzarella cheese

WHAT TO DO:

1. Mix all the ingredients together, except the warm water.

2. Add a little water at a time and knead until the dough is soft.

3. Cover with a kitchen towel and leave for 30 minutes to rise.

4. Cut into small pieces as desired and leave for another 10 minutes.

5. Roll the pieces and place in an oven tray after covering the tray with baking sheet.

6. Cover the dough with mozzarella cheese.

7. Place in a preheated oven on 180C for 10 minutes.

Tip: you can use mix of thyme and olive oil instead of the cheese.

Serving Suggestion: Serve with Hummus Dip (page 9) and Syrian Chef Salad (page 4).

Baked Artichoke

INGREDIENTS:

1kg fresh (preferable), frozen or tinned artichoke hearts

500g mixed fresh vegetables (eg peppers, carrots, courgettes) all finely chopped

1/2 tsp mixed spices

4 tbsp vegetable oil

1 tsp cinnamon

1 medium onion, finely chopped

60ml lemon juice

1L water

1 tbsp vegetable stock powder

4 cloves garlic, crushed

salt and black pepper to taste

1/2 tbsp fresh coriander, finely chopped

100g roasted mixed nuts

WHAT TO DO:

1. Preheat oven to 180C.

2. Add fresh artichokes to the vegetable stock and cook on a medium heat for around 20 minutes. If not using fresh, skip to next step.

3. Drain artichoke hearts, place in an ovenproof dish and set aside.

4. In a frying pan add the oil and the onion and stir on a medium heat until the onion is golden in colour.

5. Add the mixed vegetables and stir well.

6. Add cinnamon, mixed spices, salt and pepper, mix well and leave to cook until the vegetables are soft and browned.

7. Place the vegetables on top of each artichoke piece and place in the oven for 20 minutes.

8. Pan-fry the crushed garlic in oil until it is browned, then add to the top of the artichoke and sprinkle with the coriander and nuts.

Serving Suggestion: Serve with rice, Moutabal Shawander (page 21) and Yoghurt Salad (page 8).

Tip: You can use any mix of vegetables you prefer to fill the artichokes.

complementary dishes

Bulgur Wheat

INGREDIENTS:

250g bulgur

1 large brown onion, finely chopped

1 medium tomato, finely chopped

1/2 red pepper, finely chopped

2 tbsp vegetable oil

1/2 tsp each of paprika, dried mint, black pepper and salt

1 cube vegetable stock

3 tbsp tomato paste

600ml water

WHAT TO DO:

1. Heat the oil in a frying pan, add the onion, tomato and pepper and stir for 4 minutes or until softened.

2. To the softened vegetables, add water, spices, vegetable stock and tomato paste, and stir well.

3. When the mixture starts to boil, add the bulgur and mix well.

4. Once boiling, reduce the heat to minimum, cover and leave to cook for 30 minutes.

Rice with Vermicelli

INGREDIENTS:

250g rice

2 tbsp vermicelli, crushed

2 tbsp vegetable oil

2 cubes vegetable stock

2 cups water

salt and pepper to taste

WHAT TO DO:

1. Soak the rice in hot water for 20 minutes, then drain.

2. Heat the oil in a frying pan and add the vermicelli. Stir until it is browned.

3. Add the vegetable stock to the water and stir well. Leave on the hob until boiling.

4. Add the rice to the boiling water and stock, mix well, cover and cook on low heat for 20 minutes.

Fried Potatoes

INGREDIENTS:

500g white potatoes

500ml vegetable oil

1 tbsp thyme

salt to taste

WHAT TO DO:

1. Peel and cut the potatoes lengthways.

2. Wash and leave in a colander to drain, and season generously with salt.

3. Heat the oil in a deep frying pan until it sizzles and add the potatoes.

4. Cook until the potatoes are golden in colour.

5. Remove from the oil using a slotted spoon. Place on kitchen roll to remove the excess oil.

6. Sprinkle with thyme and salt as needed.

Flat Bread

INGREDIENTS:

500g plain flour

1 tsp yeast

1 tsp salt

125ml warm water

WHAT TO DO:

1. Mix all the dry ingredients together in a large bowl.

2. Slowly add the water to create the dough, kneading until it is smooth and even.

3. Cover with a cloth, place in a warm area, and set aside for 10 minutes.

4. Split the dough and roll pieces into small balls, place them on a tray and cover loosely. Set aside for 10 minutes to rest.

5. Dust a clean countertop with flour. Roll each dough ball into a large thin circle, around the size of a dinner plate and 1cm thick.

6. Heat a flat pan on the hob and place one piece of flattened dough at a time in to cook for few minutes. Flip the dough to cook the other side.

Tip: Can add pieces of black or green olives to the dough when mixing the ingredients.

desserts

Syrian Cake

INGREDIENTS:

560 plain flour

1 tsp baking powder

280g caster sugar

4 medium eggs

100ml milk

100 mll vegetable oil

1 tsp vanilla extract

1 tbsp lemon or orange rind

WHAT TO DO:

1. Place all of the ingredients except for the flour and baking powder in a large bowl.

2. Mix well using an electric mixer.

3. Add flour and baking powder to the mixture using a wooden spoon.

4. Grease a baking pan with butter and transfer the cake mixture into the pan.

5. Bake for 35 minutes in a preheated oven at 180C.

Tip: Serve with whipped cream and summer fruits.

Konafa

CREAM FILLING INGREDIENTS:

1 1/2 cup whole milk

1 1/2 cup heavy whipping cream

3 tbsp granulated sugar

5 tbsp cornflour

2 tsp orange blossom water

1 tsp rose water

(Alternatively, you can use
ready-prepared custard)

CRUST INGREDIENTS:

500g thinly sliced filo dough or Taze
Kadayif

2 tbsp melted ghee or butter

SYRUP INGREDIENTS:

2 cups granulated sugar

1 cup water

squeeze of lemon juice

1/2 tsp of orange blossom water

TO MAKE THE CREAM FILLING:

1. In a small saucepan, whisk together the milk, cream, sugar and cornflour until well combined and not lumpy.

2. Set the saucepan over medium high heat and bring to a boil, whisking the entire time. Continue to boil until the mixture becomes thick.

3. Remove the saucepan from the heat and whisk in the orange blossom and rose water.

4. Set the cream filling aside to cool slightly as you prepare the Konafa crust.

TO MAKE THE SCENTED SYRUP:

1. In a saucepan over medium high heat, combine together the sugar, water and a squeeze of lemon juice. Stir only until the sugar is dissolved.

2. Once the mixture boils, reduce the heat to low and cook for no longer than 10 minutes. The syrup will be slightly thicker. Stir in the orange blossom and rose water.

3. Transfer to a medium bowl and allow to cool completely before using.

TO ASSEMBLE:

1. Preheat oven to 180C. Melt butter and coat the thinly sliced filo dough with butter.

2. Grease a 20 x 30cm ovenproof dish with some of the butter. Put half of the filo dough into the dish and press down slightly. Drizzle with butter.

3. Spread the cream filling (or ready-prepared custard, if preferable) over the filo dough mixture. Place the rest of the filo dough over the cream mixture.

4. Place the dish into the preheated oven and cook for 40 minutes.

5. Pour the syrup mixture over the Konafa immediately after removing it from the oven. Serve warm.

Namora Nafishi

INGREDIENTS:

1 cup plain flour

1 cup sugar

1 cup desiccated coconut

1 cup semolina

1/2 cup yogurt

4 eggs

1 tsp baking powder

1 tsp vanilla extract

WHAT TO DO:

1. In a large bowl add flour, semolina and coconut. Mix well with a spoon.

2. In a smaller bowl add the rest of the ingredients and mix with an electric mixer.

3. Add the mixture in the smaller bowl little by little into the large bowl, mixing after each added portion.

4. Grease a 30 x 20cm ovenproof dish with butter or oil and transfer the mixture into the dish.

5. Cook in a preheated oven at 160C for 40 minutes.

Tip: Once baked, leave to cool for a few minutes, then drizzle with syrup (page 57).

Mehalabia

INGREDIENTS:

4 cups whole milk

1/2 cup sugar

1/2 cup corn flour

1 tbsp vanilla extract

pistachios or desiccated coconut to garnish

WHAT TO DO:

1. In a large saucepan over medium heat, mix together the milk, sugar, corn flour and vanilla. Stir until dissolved.
2. Continually whisk the mixture so it does not stick to the pan. It will become like a pudding in consistency.
3. Remove from the heat and spoon into small bowls. Refrigerate for 2-3 hours.
4. When ready to serve, garnish with pistachios, coconut or both.

El Mamounia

INGREDIENTS:

200g rough semolina

100g ghee

200g caster sugar

800ml cold water

1 tsp cinnamon powder

1 tsp rose water

1 tsp vanilla

desiccated coconut or mixed nuts to decorate

WHAT TO DO:

1. Melt the ghee in a pan over medium heat.

2. Add semolina and stir well for 10 minutes until the semolina starts to brown.

3. Add cold water and stir well over a medium heat.

4. Add sugar, cinnamon and vanilla. Mix well, then reduce the heat and cook for 20 minutes.

5. Stir in rose water and cook for another 5 minutes.

6. Spoon into small bowls and decorate with coconut or mixed nuts (optional). Serve warm.

Tip: You can use mixed nuts and sugar.

Sevenoaks Welcomes Refugees

How we help...

WHERE DOES THE MONEY GO?

Since we started raising money for refugee support in summer 2017 to 31st March 2022 we have spent:

£60,614

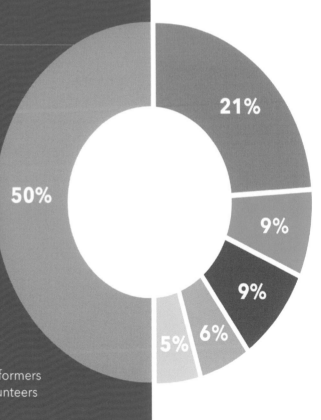

- **£30,263 (50%): Family Household Expenditure**
  Including disabled access ramp, laptops/printers and other IT equipment, driving lessons, furniture, sewing machine, garden tools, bikes

- **£12,470 (21%): Family Educational Support**
  Including tutor fees, online learning software, professional courses and exam fees

- **£3,492 (6%): Family Social Activities**
  Including train fares and tickets for social outings, swimming lessons, football courses, second-hand greenhouse

- **£5,500 (9%): Family Housing Improvements**
  Contribution to landlord's costs of preparatory work pre-arrival and ongoing routine maintenance

- **£5,752 (9%): Fundraising**
  Including flyers, posters, social media advertising, performers fees - all to raise awareness and funds, and recruit volunteers and landlords

- **£3,138 (5%): Administration**
  Insurance, accounting system, training, office and general administration

Dear Reader,

We are so happy that you get to hold this finished cookbook in your hands. Beginning this endeavour, we had little idea it would take two years, countless revisions, and endless correspondence, not alleviated by the circumstances of the pandemic. It's been an absolute labour of love, and working together with Mouna and Khaled, we have poured many hours and dedication into the final creation of this book.

We would like to thank Dr. Natalya Orme and Mrs. Ellen Douglas for running the Sevenoaks School Refugee Service Programme week after week and providing encouragement and support throughout this process. Thank you also to Alexandar for his guidance in the early steps of this process. Furthermore, we would like to thank our contacts at the Sevenoaks Welcomes Refugees charity: Georgia Shawver, Kimberly Marza, Violette Saad, and last, but most certainly not least, Humphrey Pring. Additionally, we would like to extend our gratitude to David Merewether, who made the photographs for this book. Lastly, we must thank Mouna for sharing her delicious recipes and expert guidance in developing this book.

We hope you derive at least as much pleasure from these recipes as we did in compiling them!

From the Student Team at Sevenoaks School: Harry, Georgina, Faith, Tess, Allegra, Megan, and Zenaide

Nearly all of the ingredients in these recipes can be sourced locally, however, should you need something a bit exotic, there are fantastic suppliers online that will deliver to your door. There is also a Turkish Supermarket in Orpington and a shop in Tonbridge that source all of these ingredients.

Organic Village Market Ltd
113 High Street,
Tonbridge, Kent, TN9 1DL

OTS Oriental Turkish Supermarket
334 High Street,
Orpington, Kent, BR6 0NQ